GOOD MORNING, RYAN

By Bill Morris

○ ☾ ☆

New ○ Sun Publications

Half Moon Bay, California

For information contact:

Email: newsunpub@aol.com

New Sun Publications,

227 Granelli Ave,

Half Moon Bay, CA 94019

"To Ryan, and, of course, with love to Kristin."

Preface

Many years ago, I wrote a book about your sister. A short book about how happy she was, and lessons we were learning, when she was only five.

I never imagined that years later, more years than it takes to grow a palm tree taller than our house, more years than it takes to grow an apple tree so full of apples in our backyard that I have to prop it up with stilts, and many more years than we have cats in our house (three), or happy people on our summer-time couch (four), that you would be you (five).

And now you're a happy little girl. And there are more lessons for us to learn.

So, as you run past, your hair flying, your yell yelling, your happy kid-hop hopping, hiding sneaky "andacondas" in our bed, and putting dynamite in my pants, well, I have to say to you: Good morning, Ryan.

Your Dad

3/11/2009

GOOD MORNING, RYAN

Content

Heart's Desire

You are perhaps the most photographed girl in the world. Your mother has single-handedly photographed every vision of you, I'd say down to the molecule.

There are pictures of you in purple sunglasses, snoot in the air, a starlet at five. Pictures of you in diapers, pictures on swings, standing before the Eiffel Tower, dancing the Nutcracker in a blue doughnut tutu, your face filled with a supreme look of grace, pictures of you on pumpkins, picking Easter eggs like flowers, pictures of you skipping, frowning like a grey day, laughing in a sunny park breeze, riding ponies as if you were a rajah on the back of an elephant, asleep like a toad in your bed, pictures, pictures, pictures.

So, what's up with that? Why so many pictures, why you?

Well, years ago, more than the five that you almost are right now, your mother had a dream. She dreamed her heart's desire. She was brave and dreamed a dream that didn't really seem possible, a dream that very

1

likely might not come true. And she thought about this dream, and planned the vision, and walked slowly toward it—a blind person just hoping to get there, but feeling sunshine on her face leading the way.

And she had to risk everything for her dream. Because that's the way life is, sometimes you have to give up the things you have to get to a new thing, a new thing deep in your heart. But she'd risked her life before, and saved herself before. And so she did again. Your mother is brave that way, and smart, and determined, and she wasn't afraid to walk deep into the forest alone. Looking for you.

And so I met her in the forest. A dark forest, where there's worry, unlooked-for pain, undeserved suffering, where people can lose their way, and sometimes lose their lives. And in my troubles, I could see her dream and how deeply she needed it, and being friendly, I said I'd help. And that led me to love her. And we decided to both look for you.

And it wasn't easy to bring you out of that forest. It required heartbreak and loss, bouts of joy, enduring worry about the possible, trips to hospitals sour and cold, tears, humiliation before prim white uniforms, and finally—a first picture of you, in your mother's tummy, looking more like a stubby doll than a coming baby.

And after that first picture, well the avalanche ensued. Pictures of you at every angle, pictures of you at six-month birthdays always wearing the same cone partyhat with fluffy pom pom, pictures of every friend, relative, happy grandparents holding you with surprise and joy, just more pictures of you than grass blades in the lawn or sand at the beach.

And when you go for your heart's desire, sometimes you get it, sometimes you don't. And when you do, you want to remember it, maybe take a photo or two. You know? Because every picture of you is a picture of your mother. A picture of her heart.

A Sharer and A Borrower

Right now, you are a sharer and a borrower. You have learned to share your toys with little visitors. Of course, at first that's hard, to have a toddler take your favorite floppy thing out of your hands, and maybe even drool on it! Horrible.

But you share. You sit quietly and let another person play with your lovely things. Things you love to play with. And your look is more a look of concern, not really a look of frowning begrudging. You're just doing your best and, sometimes, you're even smiling about it. You're learning to open your heart, just a little, just a little, about the amount it takes to open the door to see if the morning sunshine is coming in. You're learning to let others in. And sometimes, you'd like to just slam that door. And not let anyone play with you. But you don't. And that is my big hope for you. That you'll be a good sharer of yourself with the others around. It leads to a lot of fun and play, and even a big gift: friends.

On the other hand. You like to borrow toys. In return for sharing your things, you expect others to let you come into their house and pick out stuff from them. When you leave a good friend's house, you like to ask if you can borrow something that you like. And it's a big trial for the other little person to figure that out. Should I, do I have to? And you expect that they should. If you share, you have a right to borrow. Or at least that's the way you think.

And yes, I'm uneasy with the borrowing, even though the mothers all think it's just fine. Taking another person's happy toy when she might not want to risk it, well, that makes me uncomfortable, probably by the amount that it might make your little friend feel uncomfortable. I know it's a kind of ritual that you and your friend both participate in. It might be a sign that you each trust each other enough. But it's a risk. A risk that you might be taking more than the person wants to give, a risk that you might not return it when it's needed. A risk that you might not see another person's need, no matter how small.

I can be a sharer. I have no problem offering more than I should give. But a borrower, I'm not sure I'm as confident in myself as you. Perhaps I should learn that a borrower and a lender you can be, with enough confidence in yourself. But it's easier for me to give, than risk a take. I hope you'll be a good borrower. A person who takes but always gives back.

Herd Your Horses

You like to play a game called Herd Your Horses, a board game in which you roll a die, collect card horses, and have adventures. You like to greedily collect as many horses as you can get, because the person with the most horses when you enter the final Green Valley wins. You like to play this game, and you tell me proudly you are good at it. If you land on the right spot, you get to draw a new horse card to keep. If you land on another spot, you have to read an adventure card and take your chances. Sometimes you fight another stallion and win a horse. And sometimes, the ice comes early and foraging is tough, and you lose a horse, or a baby foal dies from being born too early. In those cases, I usually change the card and secretly read you a result that, guess what, gives you another horse. (Because that's my job.) And somehow, you always win with the most cards. Even though, when you count your herd, horse fourteen is always followed by horse eighteen, but we'll work on your counting skills later. This game is about greed and happily getting the most horses. And you always tell me you're good at it. Did I say that?

And you can accidentally draw two cards, Carrot Cake, who is a mule, and Bright Eyes, who is a donkey. And these cards don't count as horses. They're worth nothing—ol' Carrot Cake and Bright Eyes. And we secretly love them for it.

Earrings

You are sparkling clean after your bath, sitting on the rug with a little teepee of a green towel around your shoulders. Your mother is working on your hair, brushing the wet ropes into a smooth wide ribbon. Before you is a little box of old jewelry, a handful of your mother's earrings, a puka shell necklace, a beaded snake necklace, and many other shining goodies that you are picking through like cookies.

I clip two topaz earrings to your ears. You go to the closet-door mirrors to see.

You stop and stare. You see something new. And as you look in this mirror, I see back through this mirror through a thousand other mirrors and shiny store fronts and still ponds to many other lucky little faces, and you turn to your mother, your face full of wonder and secret satisfaction, and say, "It looks really good." And you absolutely mean it.

And your mother, sitting on the rug, bemused, in her earrings, smiles.

And I can only think this certainty, "This is a little girl."

And you have seen your own beauty for the first time.

Recipes

I don't use recipes when I cook. I come home from work and make dinner. And it doesn't make much difference what goes into the bowl first or last, it all gets mixed up.

Last night, you came in and wanted to help make dinner. And at first I didn't think there was much you could do, but then, I realized there were lots of little things you could do to help. I said, "Sure." We were making shrimp and artichokes.

So first I had you put globs of mayonnaise in three little bowls. I put the bowls on the floor for you (since you're not tall enough to work on the counters) and you spooned three pasty glops into each bowl, getting white clots stuck on your fingers like cotton. I cut a slice of lemon for you and you squirted it and then mixed it up. You looked up smiling and asked if there was more you could do.

So I cut the artichokes in half, sawing off their leathery tops, and placed them on the floor before you. I gave you the kitchen butter, and you pasted a smear across each artichoke's face. You liked doing that. Then I handed you the garlic salt and said, "Just a little, put just a little on each one," kind of knowing already. And sure enough, you poured a handful of garlic salt on the first one, and seeing the problem, put just a dash on the second. I washed off the first one, now lightly peppered with garlic stuck to the butter, and knew it would be okay.

I took the shrimp out of the microwave where they'd defrosted. You asked to do something more. You then put butter in a plate, shook down some pepper on it, then squeezed that lemon again. We melted the butter in the microwave, and then you poured the peppery grease over the shrimp. Done.

Next, we put out three plates, one for each of us, and you piled the shrimp like sticks on the plates. I explained that if you arranged all the shrimp with the tails pointing the same way, it would look nice. So you happily arranged the shrimp, turning them like dials. Then we put the mayonnaise bowls on the plates. And I cut three yellow slices of lemon for you to place as decorations.

Last, three Ritz crackers for each plate, with that white Laughing Cow cheese dabbed in the middle. I have to say, you're a good dabber. And then you placed the crackers on the plates like crisp orange buttons, good to eat.

Finally we picked the plates off the floor and put our masterpieces on the table. We were done. And I realized that although I didn't think there was much you could do, being so little, well, you'd actually made the whole dinner.

And you ate all of yours and you liked it.

And that's my recipe: two people working to cook up good things together.

Cheetos

You like Cheetos. They are crunchy little nuts of something covered in emergency-orange cheese powder. When they're fresh, they're like biting into a cheesy pinecone. When they're stale, they're like biting into a cheesy leather pinecone. You like them.

When you like something, it's fun to play with your food. So we play the Cheetos game.

It's an old hide and seek game, but one in which you hunt for hidden food. As you flap two hands over your eyes, I tip-toe a morsel around the room and hide it in

GOOD MORNING, RYAN

an unlikely spot. Atop the TV or on the sofa arm behind your mother's cup. They lie there, pretty obvious, like huge dried-up angle worms wearing orange slickers. Then you shout, "Twenty!" and the hunt begins.

During the game, you, the hunter, are guided by me, the caller. I start out by saying "warm, warm, warmer" as you traipse in the right direction. When you turn wrong, I say "cold, cold, colder...." with just the right amount of doubt.

And here are the stages you go through to find a Cheeto:

Cold

Colder

Freezing

Icicle

Iceberg! (I have to really shout "iceberg" because the hunter isn't paying attention.)

Warm

Warmer

Getting Hot

11

Hotter

Boiling Hot

Burning Up

Hot Lava! (I shout this last one, too.)

Then you pounce and pull the Cheeto out of its hiding place and wolf it down like a bird in a nest.

It's a fun game. You like to play it.

And I suppose someday, when you're off at college, or starting a new job, or on a trip around the world, I'll stoop and find an old Cheeto under the couch, and I'll look at it and say, "Hot Lava."

Your Strongest Insult

Some time ago, I made you mad. I must of done something pretty dire, because you crinkled your forehead and said in your entire meanness, "You puff of mud!"

Conversation While Making a Pie

This morning you spot ripe apples. So you ask for a basket to pick a few. I give you a purple basket and you pick five small ripe apples.

You suggest that we make a pie. I get out the bowls and pie tin and put them on the floor so you can help. We sit down and peel the apples, but you're still too little to use that American masterpiece, the steel potato peeler. I carefully shave the apples as we talk.

You say, "Those apple peels look like french fries."

I say yes.

As I cut up the apples, you pick out a peeled apple to eat. You ask for a bowl of sugar, because you bet the apple will taste good with sugar on it. I give you a little bowl of sugar and you dip it in and take a taste. You like it. You're up for experimenting.

I put flour and sugar on the apple slices. Then I let you smell the cinnamon as I put some in, then you smell the nutmeg. You say you'd like some cinnamon in your sugar bowl for your apple, but you also say politely that you don't want any nutmeg.

You dip your sugar apple in the bowl again until it has a cinnamon sugar cap. It tastes good.

We're ready to grease the pie tin. I ask you to smear on the butter. You do. It's really smeary with butter. I say you're doing a good job.

Then you ask, "Can I put butter on my apple?"

I say yes. You take a gob of butter and smear it all over your peeled apple until it's like a sweating bald man. Then you take a taste.

"Mmm, that's good," you say.

I look at you, shielding my amazement. "Good," I say.

Then you look at me and ask politely, "Can I put more butter on my apple?"

Now I know I'm deep into an interesting conversation.

"Sure," I say.

You smear on more butter until your apple is just a grease ball. But secretly you don't taste it.

We put the dough in the pie tin and the apples in the doughy crust. You're tasting along the way.

We take cookie cutters and cut two bats and two cats out of leftover dough. We put them on top of our pie, because it's almost Halloween.

You look at me and say, "I know what part of the mouth makes the pie taste good."

I have to know. "What part of your mouth makes the pie taste good?" I ask.

"It's the tongue." You are proud with knowing.

"You're right," I say.

And as you take a last taste of the uncooked pie dough, you say, "And my mouth is making an apple pie!"

The Scary Movie

Last night we watched "Jurassic Park." You love dinosaurs, the bigger the better. And so I decided you'd like this movie, although it's a bit scary in parts.

So we sat together, hip to hip, on the couch watching the people take little cars into the big dinosaur jungle. I explain it's like a zoo. We have a blanket in our lap, just in case it gets too scary and we have to pull the blanket over our heads. So far, so good.

You like the big tyrannosaurus spying the kids in the car. No blanket needed. You laugh when the long-necked "cow" dinosaur sneezes in the girl's face.

Then the evil fat guy confronts the stupid dinosaur that will eventually eat him, throwing a stick and saying "fetch!" Well, blanket up as the dinosaur monsterizes, popping open like an umbrella with big shaking claws and fangs. We miss some of it, but you see the monster hop in the car to eat Mr. Badguy. You get it. He's a dinosaur hot dog.

Then we have fun watching the rest of the doings. Dinosaurs running like a pack of chickens from the bigger toothier ones. Little kids being chased by raptors through a kitchen. I'm joking that the raptors like human hamburgers. That is, hamburgers made of human beans. You laugh because you know they're not human beans, they're beings.

Anyway we have a pretty good scary time, with only a little blanket diving here and there. I can't wait to tell you that there's a "Jurassic Park II." We'll get a bigger blanket.

Breakfast Suggestions

You tell your mother you don't want frozen waffles.

"Oh no," she says, "Ryan doesn't want the only thing I have for breakfast."

I say, "Would you like a cat sandwich?"

You look at me curious and shake your head no.

"Would you like a baked raccoon with raspberry sauce?"

You look at me suspiciously and giggle.

"Would you like a big slab of whale blubber?" I hold out my hands as if I'm lifting a ten-pound flour sack.

You grimace at your weird dad. You look over to your mother because she's got the real answers.

The Secret Door

You tell me there is a secret door in your closet. You want to go through.

I think a second and realize you're talking about the ceiling access hole to the attic.

You want to go up through that hole at once. You are lying in the family room with the rug pulled over you like a blanket. You're just a lump under the rug. No other part of you shows.

I say I'll show you later. It's difficult to get the attic access open, it'll take a bit of planning, moving odds and ends, and a ladder.

You want to go now. You have trouble holding your patience. A secret door is calling you. You don't want to wait.

After I finish the morning dishes, I go into the garage and get the step ladder. I open your closet door, set up the ladder, then move the miscellaneous stuff off the shelves so that you might climb up. I slide back the attic access cover like pushing a manhole cover up and over from beneath.

I go downstairs and catch you by the wrists and drag you out from under the rug. You don't know what's happening, but you're letting yourself be dragged. Your mother comes over for the fun and picks up your ankles. We carry you swinging like a hammock upstairs to your room. You're laughing as your mother and father, the cannibals, haul you away.

I show you the ladder and the flashlight on the first shelf. You're excited, you tell your mother you're going up through the secret door.

You stand on the top shelf, your head in the dark attic, looking around as if in a foreign land. You turn the flashlight around like a light in a lighthouse.

"There's a hugh pink blanket up here!" you say in amazement. You see all the pink insulation laid out across the attic rafters. You stare left and right. It's cool.

Finally, I lift you down to our level again. You're pleased with the adventure.

And I wanted to tell you, there are many secret doors in the world. And sometimes when you go through them, like now, you see the wonder.

Pumpkin Pie Tart

This morning I went to our little Half Moon Bay bakery on Main Street and bought you a small pumpkin pie. It's about the size of a tennis ball. It's a small town treat, a fist-size pumpkin pie. Good morning eating.

I bring it home in a little white sack, then place the pie on a plate. I put it on the rug next to you. You look down and like this tiny pie. It's just for you.

Later, your mother tells me that you said it was the best pie you ever ate.

If I were to write the preparation instructions, I'd write: Best eaten in Half Moon Bay.

The Mimic

Your mother laughs at me and says, "You think you're really funny, but you're not funny at all."

You chirp, "Yeah, you think you're really funny, but you're not funny at all."

Your mother and I both look down at you. We laugh.

Those little boys at preschool better watch out, the slayer is on the loose.

The Future

When I was a kid, the latest technological wonder for us was a little box that had two wheels the size of doughnuts, and a hot-dog size microphone, and you

GOOD MORNING, RYAN

could record your voice and play it back. We kids and the whole family marveled at it, even though it made you sound kind of like a parrot. And I remember getting a TV with the first remote channel changer, which started up a little motor in the TV that churned and turned the mechanical dial to change channels from Gene Autry to Roy Rogers.

And now, well, you can hold a little machine thinner than a deck of cards and it can play any song that you want to hear, thousands of them, it can talk to satellites and you can make a phone call while you drive (watch out, a new kind of accident has hit the highways), and it has a map that can always tell you where you stand in America. It makes my little two-wheeled tape recorder...well, I guess if you come out of the past wearing your old clothes, you will always look a little like a joke.

And today, you are playing on your computer. You are shopping on the internet using a game site called Bella Sara. You can buy beautiful fairy-like horses and animals, you can buy furniture and knick knacks for your imaginary website house, you can play games, and spin the wheel of fortune to win purple and green horse charms. You collect Bella Sara cards like baseball

21

cards, except you type in entry codes printed on them and get new exotic pets for your imaginary menagerie, and you get horseshoes, the currency of the imaginary realm. You are rich with horseshoes, you buy oodles of stuff online with them. At 4 1/2, you've learned to use a sophisticated computer to buy virtual prizes, you are a gleeful online shopper.

I could record my voice and sound like a parrot.

Most people will tell you you can't know the future. It's big, coming your way, and changes fast.

But I can tell your future. I know what's ahead for you. I can see it clearly in your happy heart and merry laugh. It's standing here right in front of me.

Good Morning, Ryan

I want to tell you a small part of who you are. What makes you you.

It's no secret that each night, in the dark primary numbers, your mother gets up and goes in to sleep next to you. She climbs like a mother bear into your bed, moves you over, asleep, a lump among pillows, and beds down by you. Sometimes you're drowsy, or cranky for her, sometimes you're gone, in dreamland, a warm sack of sleep, your body scrunched into a C on the sheets. Your mother climbs in and snuggles next to you. Covers to your chins, to your shoulders like a warm sea of love at high tide.

And this is a fundamental component of what makes you you. The snuggle. The warm heat of another slow-baking you. You grow in this shimmering warmth, you grow in the dark night's aura of your mother as close to you as your own pajamas.

And when you wake, you discover it's another happy day. So now that I finished doing the morning dishes and the kitchen is cleaned up, I'm next going up to your room. And I'll shine down a little extra Father light on the sleeping flowers.

Good morning, Ryan.

Big Ideas

This morning's big idea is to water the flowers in the backyard. You ask if you can. Your mother gets you the plastic watering can, turns on the hose, and you get busy. I look out the patio door and there you are carefully putting a tablespoon or two of water on the face of each rose.

Then you go over and pick two apples. You're excited because one of the apples is all red, and the other is only a little green. And they were low enough for you. You wash them with the hose, then show them to me polished and fresh.

You have the next big idea: you say, "We could make a one-apple pie!" I can guess which apple you're talking about.

Then your genius kicks in and you say: "We could put candles on it and it could be a birthday pie!"

Keep thinking, Sister. The world is getting better.

Whoa!

Sometimes you amaze even yourself. You are dressed in a Bat Girl costume, with a yellow bat emblem on your black chest, a black shirt with batty fringe, flashing a black cloak that you open dramatically like an upside down fan—a peacock show of your bat glory.

You are on the bed jumping. Mother has piled pillows and blankets on the floor at the foot of the bed. You kangaroo hop across the bed, spread your bat wings, leap high, beat your wings, and flop to the floor. It's a short flight, kind of like a dropped apple. But you're having great jumping fun, jumping off the bed with a flap or two. You're leaping like Bat Girl.

You decide that you're going to really jump high and turn all the way around in midair. It'll be a big bat spin. You step back as far as you can against the bedroom wall. You wrinkle up your nose to show you mean business, and you run and jump with all your might. You turn slowly in midair nearly all the way around, and then you thump like a dirt clod in the pillows. You jump up and shout, "I did it!" (Well almost, you only went three quarters of the way around, but it counts.)

Your face goes blank with surprise as you realize and you say, "Whoa."

Secrets

You are asked the age-old question: What do you want for dinner?

You give the proper ageless response: I don't know.

A few minutes later, your mother asks you what you want for dinner again, and then leaves the room, letting me handle it.

You look at me and say, "I know what I want for dinner. Rice with chocolate syrup on it."

"Okay."

And you add, "But we won't tell Mama about the chocolate syrup."

"Okay," I say. You check to see if we have chocolate syrup in the refrigerator. But we don't. I say, "Okay, I'll put chocolate ice cream on it."

"Okay," you say. Then you have another secret idea, "And some whipped cream."

We agree that's the recipe.

I boil rice for three.

I put rice with teriyaki meat in one bowl for you. Then I put rice in another bowl and spoon on some chocolate ice cream, with a slurp of whipped cream from the aerosol whipped cream can.

I put both bowls in front of you as you watch TV.

When mother comes in the room, you tell her the secret.

My secret is that I see you eating out of both rice bowls. Dinner is served.

(And I expect your mother's secret is that she knows you can't keep a good secret from her for more than a minute.)

Apple Seeds

I'm writing this so that you can remember lessons that you've learned. So that maybe someday, when you're feeling distant from yourself and wondering, you can look back and see some of yourself, how you were, and the lessons you knew. But often, I find I'm writing about the lessons I learn from you. Just as I learn lessons from your sister.

Your sister recently risked everything she loved to achieve the goal of the thing she most loved. She loves playing softball and her goal was to be a pitcher for a major California university team. She had worked hard and succeeded, but now she had to risk not playing ever again to achieve her goal. And she took her courage and perseverance and risked it. Now she's the starting pitcher for a California university team. And I learned from her that it's all right to take risks with the things you love to achieve the goals of the things you love.

Last night I was eating an apple that I picked from our tree as you sat beside me on the couch. We were reading a book about dinosaurs together. As I finished my apple, you asked me what the core was. I pointed to the middle of the apple and said it was this part, it has the seeds in it. I broke the core in half to show you the seeds. You're excited and you ask me to give you the core, and you pick out the seeds with your fingers, glistening black from the sweet white meat. You say, "Let's go plant them!"

And as I think of Johnny Appleseed, I realize I'm happy with your impulse to see the new seeds of things and want to plant them right away.

Lesson learned.

Mashed Potatoes

We are having breakfast, eating our doughnuts and watching "Jurassic Park III."

You say, "I love 'Jurassic Park III'."

You tell me your favorite part is when the Spinosaurus, the biggest and scariest one, rushes onto the runway to gobble up a terrified mercenary. Yum.

You're drinking your chocolate milk and watching the dinosaur eating people left and right. The heros are stuck in a crashed airplane in a tree and the old Spinosaurus grabs the pilot and gives him a quick gobble.

I pretend to be the Spinosauraus, and I growl, "I love eating human beings."

You laugh and say, "Yeah, they taste like mashed potatoes."

I think about that and yeah, they probably do.

At Your Beck and Call

You are upstairs working on your projects in your room. Your mother and I are downstairs working at our computers.

You shout down, "Tape!"

I look at your mother and say, "What?"

She says, "She's calling for something."

"Tape!"

I hear what you shout this time.

Your mother says, "You can come down and get it."

You shout, "I'm upstairs!"

I shout, "I'm downstairs!"

I get up to get the tape. I walk it upstairs. As I walk into your room, tape in hand, I shout critically, "Am I your slave?"

"Yes!" you shout.

There was no hesitation at all.

The Joke

You can make jokes and pretend. You like laughing. When you are watching "Tom and Jerry" with your friend, seeing the cat and mouse critters bopping and flattening each other with a rolled newspaper, you both throw your heads back and laugh, rolling on your rears.

And at night, you look out the patio glass door and say, "We have visitors." And usually there is one, two, three, maybe four...or even ten raccoons. Just short of a herd. They come up and put their faces against the door looking in. Your mother can't resist feeding them loads of cat food. She makes individual piles spaced by several feet, so those old raccoons don't fight each other as they paw up the kibble. They squat like aborigines around a campfire. We watch them fascinated, even though our angry cats come and spit on the glass at them.

And this morning, while your mother is on a walk, you ask me in your secret voice for some paper. I give it to you. You say you're going to make a joke on your mom. I come down later and there are two raccoons taped to the window. You've drawn, colored, and cut out two nice raccoon replicas and taped them with their noses pressed to the window, waiting for your mom.

I look at them and think of your mother coming in and seeing these paper raccoons silently waiting for her. It's a good joke.

Surprise Party

This morning you want me to get you up early. So I come in and we go make some coffee for your mother. Then, while she's in the shower, you tell me you want to make a surprise birthday party for your mom this morning.

We need balloons. We sit on the kitchen floor and blow up four or five big colored balloons and leave them grazing on the kitchen floor.

You want to go to the store and get her roses. But it's early. So we go out in the backyard with our scissors and snip five nice roses from our bushes, and put them in a little vase. They look nice, full of leaves. You want to put a gift ribbon on the vase, so we find a bright red one. It looks kind of like an ear stuck on the vase. We put these delicious roses in among the balloons on the kitchen floor.

Next you draw a big picture of your mother's favorite dinosaur, the ankylsaurus, and I help you spell "Happy Birthday Mama" on the white sheet. You take a careful ten minutes coloring this thankful ankylsaurus green for your mom.

You put the happy picture among the roses and balloons on the kitchen floor. You go up to get your mother. I know she'll be surprised because her birthday isn't for two months.

Coming in the kitchen, your mother is surprised and says, "Well, Ryan!"

Then you top it off by saying the perfect thing. Although your mother is in her mid-forties, you happily say, "Happy birthday, Mama, today you're twenty-two."

Your mom laughs delighted. It's her half-off birthday party.

The Big Red T-Rex

You're having a dinosaur birthday party. You're excited. It's a good thing.

Your mother has bought you an inflatable dinosaur for the party. She thought it would be about knee high, a fun thing, the size of a lamp, for you to move around.

But it's way more than that. We get out our trusty red balloon pump and pump for 15 minutes. It grows slowly like bread dough. When it's blown up completely, you're amazed. It stands three feet higher than you are. You have to look up at it.

You love it. You dance in excitement beside it. You quickly draw it a life-like picture of meat to eat, complete with a ham bone in the middle.

It's a kid thing to be so entranced by a new thing. A thing so cool you have to move it and dance around it. It's a sacred state of being young, of being little, and finding it's a great new world with extra cool things waiting for you.

It's a Big Red T-Rex world. And I hope it always is for you.

The Beard

You are licking the bowl. We've made chocolate brownies and you're finishing off the mixing bowl and spoon. Your chin is gooey with chocolate batter. When you look up, you have a chocolate goatee. You don't seem to notice or care at all.

Toe Art

Mama is out, so we're fooling around in the family room, where you draw pictures, do puzzles, and we play games. You have two shoe boxes full of felt tip markers. All sizes and colors, and it's often a puzzle to figure out which cap goes on which.

As the TV plays in the background, you decide on a little project.

I see you working as if you're trimming your toenails.

When you're done, you show me. The top of each bare foot has a happy face drawn on it, one green, one blue. And each toe has a little happy face on it, five little green faces and five little blue faces.

You tell me, pointing to each foot, "This one is the Mama (green) and this one is the Daddy (blue) and these are the girls (green toes) and these are the boys (blue toes)."

Okay. I see this toe art and think it's great.

Your feet have a big family.

Waking Up on Sunday

I walk into your room this morning. You are both still in bed together. You are awake, but your mother is dozing. I sing an ancient song I heard once when I was a boy:

"Good morning, good morning,

The best to you each morning.

K-E-Double L-O-Double-Good,

Kellogg's best to you."

It's an old television jingle I heard once when I was little, like you. And its happiness with morning life has stuck with me for over 50 years.

Your mother is dozing, trying to sleep in on Sunday morning, but it isn't working as I clamber into bed beside you. We're in a clump in our pajamas under the covers, you and me laughing and fooling.

You're crawling over your mother and kicking me kind of hard, but playful, because you still think I'm indestructible. We're playing around, and your mother, trying to keep her eyes shut, says, "Ryan is letting me sleep in until nine." I look at the alarm clock. It's five minutes to eight.

I tell you that your mother really likes kisses on the ear to help her sleep. I pull back your mother's hair and you give her a nice noisy kiss with lots of lip squeak. Your mother tries hard to doze on, but she's smiling. You give her a couple really big ear kisses, each noisier than the last.

I say, "Ryan, don't disturb your mother."

That makes your mother laugh out loud. But she nestles down determined to sleep on.

You have a brilliant idea. You whisper to me that you're going to change the clock. You get the alarm clock off the dresser and you studiously turn the hands to five-minutes-to-nine. (With just a little help from me.) You laugh at your own joke as you put the clock back.

Then you decide you want to have mashed potatoes for breakfast, and we leave your mother, the sleeping actress, to doze on deep into another Sunday morning.

And I hope a little of this happiness with morning life will stick to you, too, forever, like an old unforgettable song.

That Color

We drive through our neighborhood and we often discuss the color of a certain house.

You say, "My daddy likes avocados. But he doesn't want to live in one."

Well, That's Adult Help For You

Last night you stood up a couch cushion in the hallway like a high hurdle. You ran hugely determined down the hallway and jumped all the way over it. It's the height of your waist, so that was a good jump.

Your mother tells you it was a good jump. You come to me to show me. I look and it seems high. You charge down the hall and jump all the way over.

I'm pretty amazed. I say, "Wow, I didn't think you could do it!" And at that instance I think, wow I'm not expressing my confidence in you.

And the next three tries, you can't do it. You're only half committed and you stop like a balking horse before each jump.

Boy, don't let adults take your glory away from you that way. Not even your Dad.

You could do it, I saw you do it, then with one little thoughtless comment, you couldn't: Gah. Dumb Dad.

Don't let anyone take anything away from you like that. It happens all the time.

You can do it! I saw your glory! You can do it. It's who you are.

And two days later, I set up a couch cushion low so it's an easy jump. And you jump it. And then I set up two low ones, and you jump both. And then I set up one low one and one high one, and you jump both. And your glory is back.

You can jump that high cushion without thinking about it.

Good for you, High Hurdler.

Playing Rough

You and I like to play a bit rough. You jump full weight on my stomach, your teeth clenched. I usually curl up dramatically, as if a cannon ball punched me. We play fight, you poking at me with your clenched fist, not really able to hit me other than a small stab here and there. You're careful. But we like horsing around on the sofa. You jump off the sofa back, falling on me like a bird of prey. I push you slowly off the couch until you plop on the floor. And you jump back up for the next attack.

I come from a big family. So I like to quote the number one rule of horseplay to you, "When horsing around, someone always gets hurt. Just make sure it isn't you."

Overboard

There was an old poet, Blake, who wrote that you can't know what is enough without learning what is too much. For me, it means you may have to do wrong to learn what is really right. You may have to eat or drink too much to learn what is enough, when to stop.

You may have to love too much to learn to love the right amount. We're doomed to error and learning. It's who we are.

This weekend was your birthday party. And I worried that we were kind of going overboard. Twenty kid friends were invited, and parents, and it was going to be a full house. Twenty rowdy 5-year-olds at a party? It was going to be a circus, my fear. But your mother is a planner and a celebrator so the party was on.

We cleaned the house for two days. We cleared the furniture to make room. You'd think we were getting ready for a bull-fight in our living room. The hatches were battened.

There were toys for kids to play with throughout the house, like baited traps. There were tables of hors d'ouerves for adults, drinks in an overflowing ice chest, chicken platters, chips, summer sausage, bread, you name it. A kind of bounty decided on in advance. The house was shaggy with decorations, balloons, and dangling ribbons.

And when the kids and families came, it was all happy greetings. And play. And chatting and food. And Rosie, the kid entertainer, came to play games and lead the circus of kids in a cavorting circle of dancing and funny stuff. Mid-party, she led you all in single file like convicts into our house for cake and drinks, funny little dwarf convicts walking hand-on-shoulder in a waving happy line. And at that moment, I knew the party wasn't too much, it was just a happy time. Happy kids, happy parents, your mother pleased, and you excited. Then a really big chorus of "Happy Birthday." And as they sang it to you, you circled by a big crowd, you looked like a president surrounded by an inauguration. And you withstood it calmly and were the Birthday Girl.

It wasn't too much. It was enough. And that's how it works. You have to be willing to risk too much to learn what is enough. The full measure. And if you get muddled into too much, you can always learn and cut back later.

Spike

At your age, happiness is pretty simple, and delicate, and I, as an adult, watch it with amusement and ill-ease. Your wants are so open and honest, it would be easy to bruise them. And your happiness is so easy, thrilled and childish, but in a good way, that I want you to keep it as long as you can.

Your heart was into getting a robot dinosaur named Spike. You'd spotted him on TV. He seemed cool. A big dinosaur you could make roar and walk around.

And, so, for your special birthday present, we made Spike happen for you. Surrounded by too many presents from family, you pick out the box that your heart was hoping for, and sure enough, it's Spike. You're enchanted, gleeful.

It's a tussle and some assembling to get him out of the box. Then an eternal wait for the battery to charge up enough to get this monster running.

But when you finally turn him on, he's a real robot. He flashes lights like a runway up his back, he rears and roars like a miniature bear, he snaps, he coughs, he hiccoughs, he sniffs and snorts. He lumbers along like a drunk raccoon. You at the controls are learning to drive him. And he's pretty cool, and what you really wanted.

Me, I wasn't sure. I didn't know if you'd play with him for five minutes and then the disappointment set in. Who knows what something really is until you're right next to it, and your imagination is ready to fire as you press the magic button that makes it come alive.

You liked Spike. He was a good toy. One so cool that you secretly wished your friends would come and see him right away. Your heart had something precious for you that you timidly wanted others to see and want as well.

So, isn't there joy and sadness in that? Isn't there? Your joy that you at five suddenly have something you really want, and the sadness of adults who see you wanting it, and want you to have that happiness for as long as you can. And Spike's sadness that he will always be a cool toy, even after we grow past him.

Games

You have three special games that you like to play with your father.

One is "Squirt Bottle." This is a shrieking and running game. You get a plastic spray bottle and fill it with water. Then you run and squirt me in the pants as I run around the house, shrieking like a banchee. I jump, I do Keystone Cops slides around corners, I stomp and yell as I grab the damp seat of my pants. Then I turn and shout, "Give me that!" and I grab the squirt bottle from you. And it's your turn to run and shriek. It's payback time! And we squirt and run around until I'm tired. You don't get tired: you just like to squirt.

Another game we play is "Obstacle Course." This involves me taking all the sofa cushions, pillows, and ottomans and piling them up in a wobbling trail around the family room. I challenge you to jump from cushion to cushion without falling in the hot lava. I make the distances between the cushions just far enough to be challenging for you, so that you have to run, jump, and splat on the next cushion, while I shout warnings about falling in the hot lava. I build several different versions of cushion obstacle courses, and sometimes we make a wobbly mountain that you try to walk across like a trapeze artist on a cargo rope, three cushions piled directly on top of each other, tippy as a sailboat in high wind, and you usually topple off. And sometimes, I shake the cushions to make sure.

The third game we play is "Kick the Pillow." In this game, you lie on the bed on your back with your feet in the air as I throw pillows on top of you. As a pillow comes down, you kick with both feet. Sometimes you kick the pillow off the bed and sometimes it plops on your face. During the game, I throw pillows as fast as I can. You try to kick them as fast as you can. If you kick a pillow in a small flop, I say, "Not good!" and throw another pillow. If you miss and the pillow flops on you, I shout, "Terrible!" And when you succeed and launch that pillow high off the bed back at me, I shout, "That was a monster!" And you laugh and laugh. You like kicking the monsters.

And I just flop a steady rain of pillows on you for minutes at a time. Until you can't frog kick any more. And every time I shout, "That was a monster!" you can't stop laughing. Some fun.

How Much?

Our plan for you was to let your mother stay home and take care of you until you're five, ready for school. To give you a good and happy foundation of being taken care of at home. I'd seen this worked well for your older sister, who's a strong and happy person, so I wanted that for you, too. Both your mother and I did.

And last night, now that you're five, you came down after your bath, ready for bed, and said that you wanted to give me a big hug and kiss. I bend to hug you and as you plant a big squeaky one on my cheek, I say, "I love you, Ryan."

And you laugh and say, "I love you to the Moon!"

Mission control, we have landed.

Shots

It's good to tell you of the nice things about being five, but I also need to remind you about the unfortunate things. Like going to the doctor's to get shots.

It's terrible, you sit in a kind of a grey room waiting, with your mother there trying to be with you, but you really feeling kind of abandoned. The nurse comes in with her clipboard and weighs you and tries to be nice. Your mother keeps talking to you. Things seem okay.

Then the doctor comes in and tries to be nice to you. He sits and talks a bit, but very soon, he gets to work. He puts the magic coin on your bare chest and the tongs in his ears and listens, as if you were a radio. He pushes this and prods that. He looks in this part and that part with his secret scopes. It's uncomfortable. He looks down at his little checklist, I'm sure, and checks off the box beside, "Appropriately miserable."

Then because the regular nurse is out today, he gets ready to give you shots. You don't want to. He gives you one—and then has more! And then you've had enough. You start to struggle and protest as he tries to give you another. You valiantly cry and struggle as best you can. Until the doctor is blinking and upset, because he doesn't have a recipe that takes away fear, that cures lack of control, that takes away the maladies of worry and suspicion. Until, after the ordeal for both you and him (and your mother), he tells your mother to be sure to come next time on a Monday, when the shot-giving nurse is there.

I'd call that a draw, Ryan. And I declare you healthy.

The Christmas Ladder

You ask me to go get the highest ladder we have. We are decorating the Christmas tree, stringing the bare branches with new lights, and you want to launch the star on top of the tree. You need the highest ladder to get up there.

I go and get the big ladder, ten foot. I stand it up beside the tree like someone working with a flag pole. You're looking pretty eager about getting up there.

You start to climb step by step. You get to the top two steps and Claire and I have to make you stop. You turn and sit on the second-to-the-top rung beside the tree. You tell me to call you Pippi, after the first Swedish-little-girl-super-hero, Pippi Longstocking. You know, the one who lifts horses and throws bullies into trees? The one with the excellent, unforgettable red braids that reach out like arms?

Earlier, you asked Claire, 22, to jump up and down. I tell Claire that you are projecting the things you really want to do in your excitement about Christmas decorating.

You sit atop the ladder looking down with the Christmas tree beside you. You look down on your family. You sit illuminated by Christmas lights in a dark room. A room strewn with Christmas ornaments and decor everywhere. And I can tell you like what you see.

Dancing to the Banjo

Last night we went to visit some friends for Hanukkah dinner. We lit the first candle of Hanukkah, and they told the old story about the burning oil that lasted for days, like the fish from a basket that fed thousands. Everyone has miracles they like to believe in.

Than after dinner, two friends played, one a guitar and the other her banjo. You take to the center of the rug and do your best ballet moves. You are wearing a white slip as a dress, your arms are moving like slow wings, and your tip toes are up, and you're twirling and twirling in ballet. You literally twirl 30 or 40 times in a row, until I'm sure you're going to fall down, and you do. Then you get up and twirl another 30 or 40 times. You're really dancing.

And what you don't know is that my grandfather played the banjo. And maybe somewhere back in your genes you can hear my granddad's banjo and know its for dancing. Not many people would think of dancing ballet to the banjo. But you do. And it's enough for me to remember my granddad. And that's how history comes back to us. The children bring it.

Compliments of Christmas

You spend a bountiful Christmas of many many presents heaped on you, as a daughter, granddaughter, sister, niece, friend. You're feeling good.

Your grandfather, a retired military officer, is trying on his new grey bathrobe on Christmas day. And you say, "It looks really good on you, grandfather, it matches your hair!"

And he laughs. He thinks that's funny. And he says, "Perfect, Ryan."

Proud Morning

This morning as we sleep, you get up and go downstairs by yourself. It's 7:30 and the house is quiet. You walk down the stairs and meet Gypsy, our fluffy grey longhair waiting, meowing like a rooster.

By yourself, you go and get a cat bowl. You fill the bowl with cat food. But Gypsy, the snobby mistress, walks away to the back door. You follow and let her out.

But like an obstinate cat she doesn't go out. She stands and just looks out. Like a cat.

You pour two more bowls of cat food, one for each of the other cats. And then Gypsy comes and eats. The house is still quiet. Your mom, Claire, and I are sleeping upstairs. You think of the next thing to do.

But then Gypsy wants out again, and so you open the front door and this time she strides out like a model at a fashion show.

You wash the cat dish. You use soap and it makes suds. You aren't sure you got all the suds off the dish after you wash it.

Then it's time for your breakfast, so you come back upstairs and pat my foot. I wake up and you tell me proudly about your morning chores, how you fed Gypsy by yourself, and washed the dish, and let Gypsy out, but she wouldn't go, and then she did go. And now its time to make breakfast.

And I say, "Very good, Ryan." I realize you've been downstairs by yourself in a big house alone, doing work you think you need to do. Helping out.

I'm pretty impressed. Amazed actually. Such progress as a person, only five. And I'm proud. Literally proud to tears.

Nice job, Ryan. And to top it off, you're happy this morning.

So we go downstairs, start a fire in the fireplace, and roast a hot dog for breakfast.

This day has had a really good start.

Up to Here

I fix you pancakes and bacon and hot chocolate with a squirt of whipped cream.

You watch your morning cartoons.

A half hour later, when I pick up your tray, it looks like you haven't eaten anything.

I ask, "Ryan, did you eat your breakfast?"

You say yes. You put a finger to mark the top of your rib cage and say, "I ate my hot chocolate and now I'm really full up to here."

New You, New Me

You're changing fast now, I see and hear new ideas and things from you each day. I note that you can read the words "the" and "and." You can go to the bathroom by yourself. You say surprising things, like when you were puppeting your play horses around the house claiming they must jump with "style and grace." Your mother questions you about where you learned about "style and grace." From cartoons? From school? And you say proudly you don't know, you just learned it.

When I get up in the morning, my hair is usually in a rooster tail on top of my head. Kind of a comical hat, and it makes you laugh. Tonight, I come home after work, and your mother wants you to look at me. I've had a hair cut and my hair is short.

You look at me and say, "It makes you look like an old man." Then you think and that didn't sound right.

You quickly say, "It makes you look like a man."

But that isn't right either.

Then you try again and tell me, "It makes you look like a new man." You like that. You beam at me.

A new you, a new me.

Tooth Wiggling

It's late. It's time for sleep and I go into your room to check on your progress. You're with your mother and you're in the dark, no where near sleep. You have your finger in your mouth. You're checking for loose teeth, wiggling them. A friend or two has lost teeth, and you're interested. So you're pushing on molars still planted rock-hard and saying you think they're loose. According to you, a good handful of your teeth are loose. You're looking forward to putting the loose pioneers under your pillow for the tooth fairy. I'm amused that what I know to be a kind of fearful and sometimes gruesome event has you eager and excited. For you, it's kind of like mining for future gold, but for me with my own gold back in my mouth, it's funny that you're even prospecting. But it's okay to do a little harmless wiggling (and hoping) for now.

Saturday Morning

It's going to be a busy morning taking down Christmas lights. Each is busy in their morning routine. And at this stage we're all busy in the bathroom.

I'm naked in the shower. I look through the steamy door and your mother is dressed in jeans, wearing a pink shirt, leaning over the counter into the mirror, doing her hair.

I call out, "You look pretty in pink."

Your mother laughs.

You say something and your mother asks me if I heard you. As I get out of the shower, toweling off, she tells me you said that you look beautiful in pink.

I look around the corner and you're sitting on the toilet, naked, with a book in your lap.

I laugh that we're both naked and say to your mother, "You're definitely in the bathroom with two Grouts."

You mother says that's for sure.

And you look over and say, "I look *lovely* in pink!"

And I say, "And you look lovely on the toilet."

Balloon Rocket Science

We are in the field, inflating long balloons using a hand pump. Then you pinch them off and point them toward the sky. They fly off with a long weeeeeeeee. You think it's so funny. You run across the field in your pink boots to pick them up again.

We're blowing up another to let go flying. It pops! We're both blinking.

You laugh and say, "That was in-expected."

I laugh, too (because of what you said.)

You think it's so funny how the balloon popped and surprised us. You jump with your heels in the air to show me how it popped.

We take our balloon rockets into the house because it's cold in the field.

Now we're flying them zig-zagging like flies around the living room. They zip and zoom in surprising directions. You can't stop laughing. You're laughing your head off like a runaway popcorn popper.

Then a rocket swoops to the 20-foot ceiling and sticks to a cobweb in the skylight. It's hanging like an icicle. We both wonder how we're going to get it down.

I let you think on it.

You say, "We need a long stick." You run and get a short stick, a three-foot piece of broom handle. I explain that we need a longer one by pointing at the balloon nearly 20 feet overhead. Our stairs lead to the skylight, and you think and say, we need the broom. We go and get it, and I climb the stairs, reach high, and can just brush down the errant balloon.

You jump on it with glee as it hits the floor. I'm realizing that you immediately solved the problem by thinking of a tool. With images of middle-aged monkeys calmly slurping termites off a stick, I realize that at five you are way smarter than a chimp. You may be destined to be a balloon rocket scientist.

Service

I need to tell you something about myself. A little thing. I have an exaggerated sense of having to supply, to serve, to feed. I don't know exactly why, but I know of my father's steadfast service to my family. And so I suppose somewhere it may be built in.

If you're hungry, I need to feed you. I cook a meal, and if it isn't good to you, I'll make another. I remember your sister Claire's lunch bags for school were always stuffed with things to eat, literally stuffed round as hippos full of goodies, crackers, candy, celery, chips, rolls, fruit, and good things. Way beyond what was normal. She spent most of her time sharing her lunches rather than eating them.

I need to help. So much that I can intrude. But it's my way of making sure you believe in a world that will meet your needs. Provide what you need. You can dream and have what you dream about.

And so, in the same way, I feed the cats. Gypsy wakes up at 7 every morning and I have to get up and feed her. I put food out for Grey Boy, the stray cat that comes to our house each morning. And sometimes he eats breakfast twice. Your mother and I put out food for the raccoons. Not just a cup of kibble, but pounds of the stuff slewn across the deck, enough to feed the three, and sometimes five raccoons that come and look into our windows with expectants gazes. They're seeing in with a vision of hope.

And that's me. And after feeding the raccoons, I admit to you (and myself) "I am an animal feeder."

And you laugh and say, "But you're not an animal tamer!"

And that's right. I'm not taming anything. I'm just feeding my own wild animals so they can be free.

Bliss

A wise man and a scholar, Joseph Campbell, believed you should follow your bliss. That means that as you follow your life, you should do the things that make you feel good, feel fulfilled, do the things that are important to you. Follow the things that excite you, follow your bliss.

Your sister does that. She loves to play softball, and that's what she's doing. She's played softball with all her heart, in fun and in pain, all the way up through college. And she went to college to play softball, to follow her bliss. Other people might think it's more important to get an education in college than to play softball. But for your sister, playing softball is more important, and so she's getting an education as she does it. And on the way, she's won awards, been president of a student service organization doing good works, won money in scholarships, got good grades, received recognition as a student scholar, published softball articles writing a column in a national softball magazine, and lived hard in happiness as she won and in pain when she lost. And the reward was and is doing what she loves.

That's a kind of following your bliss. And many people live differently. They aim their lives at earning money, or gaining fame, or becoming powerful and dominating others; some aim at being beautiful and having beautiful things. Some ache for love. Some want to be soldiers. There are just many other types of goals that people can go for. Other than living for the thing you love, your bliss.

And a man once asked Joseph Campbell what happens if you follow your bliss. He was wondering if that's the secret to being successful and making lots of money and having all the things you want.

And Joseph Cambell smiled and said simply, "You attain bliss."

The Death of Fear

Our house has steep stairs. There are probably 14 carpeted steps to the upstairs landing. Enough stairs that I've always worried a bit about you, as a toddler and now as a 5-year-old, tumbling down like a cardboard box. So at the top step, I always hold your hand and make sure you hold onto the banister. So we don't have any tipping accidents.

And then, last night, approaching the stairs, you showed me a new trick. You laid down on your belly at the top of the stairs. And with your hands out in front, you slid like Superman flying to the bottom of the stairs. Head first, on your belly, you slid down the stairs the whole way. You rode your body as a little bumping boat to the bottom.

And I'm not worried about you falling down the stairs anymore.

(And actually, the next day, I had to try it myself.)

The Frog

It's a grey afternoon and we've had more than enough TV. I ask you if you want to go outside and look for tadpoles. It's been a wet Spring, the puddles are full like mother frogs waiting. At first you don't want to. Then you think about it and you say, "Sure."

We get a small plastic tub with a yellow lid to see what we can catch.

We walk out with you holding our plastic tub like an Easter basket to your chest. We're talking about what fun we had last year wading in the ponds on the bluff.

I remind you that last year you fell in and stood up in water up to your waist. You laugh and remember.

We prospect for puddles across the bluff tops. We know where the best pool is to check. When we get there, the water is the color of milky coffee. No living things in sight. We move on. We check other puddles.

Then we see our first frog. I point him out, and with both of us kneeling, he hops through the grass into shallow water as we watch. You like it, it's pretty cool to see a frog.

We move off to look in another ditch. But no luck. The ditch is too steep and deep for us to check out.

Then you want to go back and see if we can catch that frog. I think and guess that he's probably back up by now. We head back for the capture.

When we get to the pool, I tell you to be quiet because the frog has seen us once and will be afraid when we come back. We sneak up on the pond. You don't see anything. But I look and sure enough, there is our frog hiding in low grass.

I quietly point the frog out to you. I say, "You want to try to catch him?" Yes! You're excited.

I creep up and put out our tub by the water's edge. Just in the right place so the frog can't jump into the water without going toward it.

And then he jumps. Right in!

I put the lid on and you're eager to look in the tub at our frog. You can't believe we caught him.

Me either, it was sheer luck.

So we walk the frog back home to show your mother. You hold the plastic tub with the little green frog in it as if you were carrying a boxed jewel at your chest.

You keep saying, "I can't believe we got a frog!"

And we take the box home and show your mother. You even unload the frog in our dry bathtub so that you can safely touch it. It's slimy. You can barely touch it with the point of your finger. You enjoy just looking at it. This is a cool hopping animal you caught.

And our little field outing is a triumph. And as you go off talking to your mom about the frog, I take it back out to its pond and release it.

You, and that frog, have had a big adventure this day.

God

Your mother tells me that they had chapel today in preschool. Your preschool is part of a church, so the pastor comes in from time to time.

I'm not particularly religious. So I'm not sure what to say.

Your mother asks you, "What is God?"

And you say, "It's what you breathe in and out."

And as a man, getting older, I don't have a word to add to that.

Breaking the Eleventh Commandment

I'm doing the morning dishes. You come in and stand quietly beside the refrigerator in your pajamas. You smiling say, "I know what I want for breakfast."

I can read your face, this is going to be good.

"What do you want for breakfast?" I say with lilting skepticism.

"Ice cream."

"Chocolate ice cream?" I ask.

"Yes."

"In a bowl?" I ask.

You just smile.

"Okay," I say. I know I am breaking one of the commandments handed down from on high, Thou Shalt Not Eat Ice Cream for Breakfast.

And I don't care. It's Sunday, God's day. Let's be happy.

And so for breakfast this morning you have a bowl of chocolate ice cream.

And I guess if I don't get into heaven, I'll know why.

Carry On

Life has its disappointments. Small failures. Others letting you down.

It's unpredictable mostly. For example, you like to swim in the hotel swimming pool when we travel to see our relatives. So, because your mother and I don't want to stand shivering in icy water to our waists, we always ask if the hotel has a heated pool. And we ask if it is actually heated. But for three hotels in a row now, the answer was always, yes the pool is heated, yes it's turned on. And in each hotel, when we arrived, we put our hands up to the wrist in shivery water. And a desk clerk explains that the pool heater is broken. It'd be days before the correct pool part comes in. Three times now.

And that's a disappointment to you. Being told it's too cold to go swimming.

But you handle it okay. You're not terribly upset. We find other things to do.

I'm mad. Mad this last time about being told four times before and after our reservation that the pool is fine when it is not. Thoughtless people are in the way. Thoughtless people saying things they think they know when they don't.

This is a characteristic of life. Others fouling up. And will you fog up your life with anger because others exist, behave this way? What do you do now?

And I think you have to be you and still be happy. Otherwise these silly people own the world. And you do that pretty well right now. So carry on.

Father in the Past Tense

Leaving for work, I walk into the family room to say goodbye to you. I bend and kiss your forehead and say, "Have a fun day, Ryan."

You say, "Bye, Dad!"

Then you say, "Bye, Did!"

You think about it and laugh. I laugh, too.

Did: the past tense of Dad.

Falling Off

I'm washing the morning dishes and you are in the next room on the couch. I hear a little commotion and you exclaim, "Dorffie!" (the name of our nosey cat). You walk into the kitchen to tell me.

"I fell off the rocking chair, then I fell off the couch," you say brightly.

I turn with suds on my hands to look at you.

You say, "Now, I'm going to the bathroom. I hope I don't fall off the toilet."

You're pretty happy on Falling Off Day.

And as you disappear into the bathroom, I say, "I hope you don't, too. Call me if you do."

That's the Story

You come to me to tell me a curious story. One of your friends wants to buy me a Star Wars Lego set. My forehead crinkles trying to understand why.

You say earnestly, "Yes, it's a Star Wars set for 58 and up." (Your mother laughs in the background.)

I suspect I'm going to see a lot of new Lego pieces around the house. And I'm not expecting them to be all for me.

Let's

I notice that when you say "Let's" you pronounce it differently, like a kid.

You say, "Yes play with my dinosaurs" or "Yes make mushy cookies."

I kind of like it. It starts with the answer you want and then the thing you want to do.

Yes make mushy cookies!

Breakfast of Champions

This morning you come in early and tell me what you want for breakfast.

You want to have a bowl of Lucky Charms and watch King Kong.

True Story

Here is a true story that I wrote:

Coyote's Curse

Little Feather wanted to be a Great Chief. But his father and mother, Stone Hands and Little Heart, had not taught him the right lessons. And Little Feather's ways were little. In battle, Little Feather led his tribe angrily, but his warriors did not count coup and did not gather great honors. Little Feather shouted and blamed his warriors. His warriors secretly said that Little Feather was not a Great Chief.

One day, Little Feather was walking in the desert speaking angrily to the rocks and hills. Coyote saw Little Feather and heard his talking. Coyote came to

Little Feather, laughed and said, "I will help you become a Great Chief!"

Coyote went to his secret home in the canyon. He took his favorite kachina and put wings on its back, and sent it flying to Little Feather.

The next morning, when Little Feather left his tent, he saw the kachina with wings standing there. And when he touched the kachina, it turned into a great warrior with wings. And the warrior said, "Coyote has sent me to help you become a Great Chief."

That day in battle, Little Feather's warriors saw the new warrior with wings and they knew he was a Great Warrior. During battle, each time they saw the warrior's wings, they took heart and fought well. They gathered much honor and counted many coups.

In the battles that followed much honor was given to the kachina warrior and to Little Feather.

But, secretly at night, Little Feather was angry. When he saw the great warrior's wings, he remembered Coyote's laugh, and thought, "Those wings are a sign that Coyote does not believe I am a Great Chief. He does not believe I can do this myself!"

One day, Little Feather went to the warrior with wings and said, "You must cut off your wings so that all can receive honor equally!"

But the warrior with wings refused. He said, "Coyote gave me these wings, they are what I am."

Little Feather returned to his tent angry. That night he snuck into the warrior's tent. He found the kachina doll and tried to break the wings from its back. But he couldn't. So he took the kachina and threw it into the canyon.

The next day, when his tribe saw that the great warrior with wings was gone, Little Feather said nothing.

But that morning, Coyote found the kachina in his canyon. He became angry.

Coyote went to Little Feather and he laughed and said, "You have thrown my kachina in the canyon. So now I give you this curse: from this moon and forever, you will be who you are and who you have always been."

And it was so.

In this story, your sister Claire was the kachina doll. Someday she can tell you what it was like.

'Til Yesterday

Up until yesterday, your hair was long. You were born with a mop of curly brown hair. And your mother was a guardian angel of your sacred hair for years. Your hair grew, went long down your back. Damsel hair in a fairy tale.

And I remember being clearly warned about not cutting it. Your long hair was important.

I laugh at this now, because kids always make mistakes with scissors. They clip a bit off here, or go behind a curtain and give themselves a quick trim. You did. Your mother had to take you to a hairdresser to get the back evened out again. Scissors fun. Many kids have it.

But yesterday you and your mother went to the hairdresser for a serious change. You and she had decided to cut ten inches off. Enough that someone who needed it might get the makings of a new wig. As you said, "To give it to a bald girl."

To you just bald, but to us, small and bald and needing.

So you had an adventure, cut your hair, and made a donation. A gift of your cut hair. And this was a good thing, Ryan. To change and to serve others.

And, of course, you look pretty cute in new shorter hair. And you were excited to show your gym class the new you.

The Long Game

You and I play a game of Battleship while mama naps.

You place your ships carefully on the Cartesian grid, hiding them from me. Next, with bingo-like accuracy, we'll call out grid coordinates and bomb each other's secrets.

I think the secret to this game is a consistent search pattern with just a little random luck. However, as I learn, you have a secret weapon that is sure to defeat me.

We start out calling numbers. I say, "B4." And you buzz busily as you check the map and say, "Misser!" You call out two coordinates, and I say, "Miss."

We call a lot of numbers. You get a few booms. I keep calling numbers, but they are always a miss. You point with one finger at the letter column, then point with your other finger to the number column, and then you say, "Misser!" happily each time.

After about 15 minutes and no results for me, I'm getting the picture. I realize this is going to be a really long game. No matter what number I guess, it's always a miss.

Because you can't really read the map. You're just reading the numbers and letters and making a guess yourself. And your guess is that I'm always wrong.

So I hurry up and let you win a little faster.

(And mid-game we have a little tutorial on reading Cartesian coordinates just for fun.)

Too Many Tomatoes

Well, we went too far last night. We decided to watch the third version of King Kong, because you like King Kong and heard there was a big snake in this one. In third version the natives aren't as scary and the ape is clearly a man walking full-height in an ape suit. I mean, the Big Foot film of a man trudging in the forest in an ape suit was more realistic.

But in this 1976 version, filmmakers are still into bloody effects. And I haven't seen the film at all. We watch Kong get semi-amorous with Jessica Lange. A little uncomfortable there, but you don't notice.

Then in the final climax, Kong is cornered on the top of the World Trade Center as Jessica is screaming to save his life and vicious attack helicopters are closing in. They're focusing high-powered mini-guns on the beast. Then they open fire.

The result is incredibly gruesome. As you watch, big batches of blood and wounds are exploding all over old Kong's poor body. You laugh! You say, "They're shooting tomatoes!"

Your mother and I are shocked at the violence and as the scene passes we don't want to clarify what was happening at all. After the movie is over, you say you really liked the tomato-shooting part.

Argh.

Quiet Easter

We had a quiet Easter. Your mother had smothered our coffee table with Easter presents for you, and your grandma and grandfather had added a handful of specially wrapped gifts. You had the excitement of Christmas as you found cool things for you.

A stuffed chimp named King Kong was waiting with bunny ears. And several books about dinosaurs and a moving pterodactyl toy that actually bit your finger with a squawk if you popped a finger in its beak.

You had fun hunting for Easter eggs. We'd planted way too many. Plastic eggs with interesting toys and go-gaws inside that you marveled at after breaking each one in half. There must have been a grocery bag full. We had to play the hot lava game to direct you to them all. In the end, it was more like Halloween with a bag of goodies than Easter.

It was a nice quiet day. Sunny and smiling. We cooked a ham and had a big dinner. You played outside in your secret garden. The parents talked. Nothing special.

Then you come in to tell us an ambulance, fire truck, and a police car have arrived two doors down. We parents kind of crisp a little, worrying that someone in their Easter party has had a heart attack. But the emergency workers are walking slowly, and after a bit the police car moves off again like a shark on patrol.

The next day, we learn that our neighbor, in a fit of glee, had jumped down the stairs and banged his head on the overhang on the way down, cut himself badly, then crashed into another partier at the stairs bottom, breaking glass and imparting more gashes and blood. So a number of people went to the hospital for stitches and came back to a cold Easter meal.

Completely different Easters, in two houses that sit almost side by side. And I guess I'd choose our world, with you and its over-abundance of gifts any time. Though I'm sure our neighbors had fun, with scars and stitches to prove it.

About the Loch Ness Monster

You're into the Loch Ness monster. You think it's a mysterious plesiosaur that haunts the lake, grinning with big teeth and a long waving neck. We've seen it many times in cartoons and movies. You think it's cool.

You're watching a Loch Ness documentary in which elderly scientists, at the end of their careers, are taking an exciting expedition to see if they can discover Nessy. These scientists had a close brush with "something" in the Loch long ago, and now they're returning one last time to see if they can find it. As usual they have five days to do it.

They've lined up boats with special sonar and underwater cameras, and they're serious, jovial, enthusiastic, and scientifically careful not to say things that will displease the scientific skeptics. And they're hopeful to find something. They are elderly, mature men, eager to find the answer to an old mystery.

The documentary talks to all the usual Nessy sorts, innocent bystanders who swear they saw it, the local retired constable who saw it once and won't go out on the lake, the local biologist who studied the loch and sees it as insufficient in nutrients to support a large animal, and skeptics and hoaxers—all have their say.

The lake is 800 feet deep and many miles long, and ends in a river outlet that eventually goes to the sea.

I realize as these men talk that they have an unexamined belief. They believe that Loch Ness is Nessy's home.

And I say, "You know sometimes when you're trying to solve a problem, you have to look at the things you believe, to understand how you see the problem.

Sometimes you believe a wrong thing, it's an assumption, and so you may not find the right answer."

You're listening. And I say, "For example, these men believe that Nessy lives in the lake, but what if Nessy or something like Nessy only visits the lake? Like salmon, they don't live in the streams, but once during the year the salmon return to their streams to lay their eggs. Maybe Nessy only comes to the lake sometimes. And because these men believe that Nessy lives in the lake, they look for it at the wrong time."

I want you to see that assumptions and beliefs can hold you back, and sometimes you need to examine your beliefs in order to find the right answers, to be free.

And you say, "Yes, I believe Nessy only comes to the lake to lay eggs!" You say this seriously.

And I realize you're parroting a belief I just handed to you. You're a little young to understand. Maybe I'll talk to you again when you're older.

And I guess the legendary Loch Ness monster is still safe for a bit longer. And after a short visit, not finding what they want, the scientists return to their homes, too. Maybe both sides having hearts that just had to return.

The Song

Today I heard you make your mom laugh.

You walk up to her and sing, "Was he King? ...Was he Kong?...Was he King Kong?"

King Kong would be proud. It surprises your mother and she laughs.

Things Best Unsaid

I want to warn you about things that may harm you later in your life. Subtle things. Unsatisfied wants, needs, blocked creativity, love that goes bad and turns to addiction. It is the case for millions. They've lost or never received the thing they needed, and so find another substitute that feels nearly like it. The adoration of fame, the love of money, the control or adrenaline high of extreme athleticism, the blurred-false feelings of love in drink, the hidden cloak of work for the workaholic, the many, many subtle forms of addiction. People desperate and in despair who cannot fulfill the things they need themselves. Because we depend on others, and others may not care, they can easily let you down.

It's a negative negative thing. And many live it. Everyday. The world is grey even when the sun is shining.

But this morning you are dancing with a pink blanket. You are waving a pink blanket like a matador as you dance and jump off the couch. You are happy and dancing.

And I hope I never have to give you the news about the rest of the world, the one outside your dance.

A Story We Don't Want to Tell

Your mother comes to talk to me about you. You were telling her a story about how you were born, starting out in your mother's tummy, and how Claire started out in your mother's tummy, too. This is a story you don't know. That your mother is not your sister's mother. I hadn't thought of this yet, but your mother has, and it's something you don't know and perhaps we need to tell.

Not all stories are good. This one, well, is perhaps the least good. When Claire was 15, her mother became sick. Truly sick. And there was nothing we could do to fix it. Claire and I spent a year of doing our best, walking cold hospital hallways trying to be brave, worried but carrying on, trying to get back to normal. Many times afraid. Crying secretly out of sight so no one would see us, trying to keep a normal life at work and school. It was terrible for Claire, and she still carries many black clouds inside her. And we did our best, at work and school, struggled, washed dishes, had a last birthday party. But it didn't do any good. And Claire's mom is gone. She couldn't help it, she never meant to leave Claire.

But that's not your story, your mom is strong and healthy, happy, and loves you truly. You can feel it. And you'll have her for a long long time. No worries. And when you have a mother like that, love her and enjoy her for as long as you can. You, Claire, your mom, and I are a new family. And each of us will have a different story. Make the one you tell a good one, a happy one. That's the real story to tell, yours.

Morning Dishes

I'm washing the dishes first thing in the morning before anyone is up, but then you walk in to talk to me. I turn to you with sudsy hands as you ask if I'll make breakfast for you. You're really hungry.

I look and see your face. It is open and honest. I feel my love for you.

"Sure, I'll make it right away."

Important Phone Calls: A Lesson

We take your sister Claire to the airport. She's leaving for Switzerland for four months. She has two tremendously heavy bags, and I can feel my arm going numb just carting them.

We hug goodbye and then Claire disappears into the security line. You, your mother, and I walk off. We are not more than ten feet away when you say, "I wonder where Claire is now."

I say, "Oh I bet she's somewhere over Mexico."

I say, "She'll probably call soon."

You say stoutly, "There are only two reasons for a phone call."

I ask, "What are those?"

You say, "If you spill your water or if it's a crash landing."

I laugh, "Those are two completely different calls. Which would you make first?"

And true to form, you say, "I'd call if I spilled my water. Then I'd call if it was a crash landing."

Lost Worlds

You want to be a paleontologist and a horseback rider. You know where you're headed.

But it's possible to become lost and not know. To wonder why you're doing something when it doesn't make sense anymore, when you've done something too long, or doing it doesn't leave you feeling good. It's possible to kind of wonder where you are and how you lost yourself.

But it's also possible to find yourself again. This is why we have those stories of lost worlds that you like so much. Worlds where few humans have ever tread, where the dinosaurs and big beasts roam free. Lost places where you must find yourself to survive. And it's dangerous. And the story is interesting when you find yourself there.

But you can also find yourself again after a simple thing. In early summer, you smell the baked pine of a cypress tree near the sidewalk. You look at the shade under the tree spelling words that you've never known. As you walk, perhaps a bee bumps into your head and flies away harmless. And you stop and look around you and see the world, beautiful and uncaring. And you leave your worries behind because you can pick them up or not later, if you want, they'll always be there, but meaningless in this story of lost worlds. And you remember that you are free. It is the world that is wonderfully lost, and you're a part of it.

New Wet Suit

Yesterday, which happened to be Father's Day, we went and bought you a new wet suit. Perfect for cavorting in our cold ocean.

So we had to go to the beach. It was a bit windy when we got to our spot on the inner harbor. A long strip of sunny sand, with other families hunched on towels, and dogs running up and down the beach like canine fools. A sea lion is safely resting under the wharf where beach walkers can come within steps of it. It doesn't mind, perhaps sick, hungry, or just resting.

The water is still with a skin of windy ripples. You and I walk out hand in hand, wading in our wetsuits. You feel how funny it is to have cold water slowly seeping into your boots and up your legs. We're kind of like mannequins. We've landed happily on another planet. We walk to where the water is clear and you can see down into it, peering at the shells and seaweed.

By now, our wet suits have done their work, our legs and feet are warm. From years of surfing, I know the water is really cold, cold enough that I don't care to dip my hands into it. But you've discovered that modern wetsuits are great. You're ready to dive head first under the water to search for shells. And you do!

You bob your goggled eyes under and see the pinkish shells. You catch great gobs of slithery-green and feathery-red seaweed for me to hold. You find flat rocks, pull them up and throw them. It's shallow enough that you crawl, crawdad style, through the water looking down on the sand bed. You raise your head and bubble burst your breath free. Then hold and look down again.

I stand beside you and comment as you explore the watery parts of our life. You're excited and having fun. At one point, in waist-deep water, you have trouble getting to your feet and start laughing as you fall over, clowning...a clown fish. At another point we see the four bald pates of harbor seals floating and bobbing, a social gathering, not far away. We walk slowly toward them to get a better look.

Think of it, something as simple as a thick rubber suit gives you a new world to play in. You the newest skindiver in knee-deep water. And later, after shucking you out of your wet suit, like pulling macaroni tubes off your arms, you sit wrapped in a towel watching TV in our family room. Just a little bit cold, but we both know it was worth it.

The Apology

You've been feeding the birds. You have a sack of birdseed that we spread out along the fence for the birds to pick up. You also scatter a bunch on the hand rail on the back deck. It's a sunny morning, cool, and a good day for feeding birds. You say, "Our backyard is a paradise for birds!"

Later I go to the glass door and see your bag of birdseed on the rug. It's turned over and has spilled a couple tablespoons of seeds into the shag. I'm going to have to pick it up, fingerful by fingerful, off the carpet. I say, "Ryan, you need to be careful with the birdseeds, they spilled on the rug." You come in to see.

You say, "Sorry, Dad." I remark at how simple and well done was your apology. I realize this is an achievement in your growing up. I'm not sure if you learned this from your mother or elsewhere, but I'm well satisfied with this simple growth.

I say, "So be careful next time." But my voice actually says, "Good job."

Fourth of July

For the Fourth, we're going on a boat ride. A friend is holding her 50th birthday on board a small yacht for a cruise on the Bay. We arrive at the wharf an hour early and look at a huge boat that is sleek and shapely, like an athlete wearing sunglasses.

You're busy spotting sea gulls. We eat a little, then we wait some more and our friends arrive. We learn that the boat isn't the big sleek one. It's the littler one behind it, a chunky two decker, a little older, a little more wobbly. Your mother thinks about sea sickness on this smaller craft.

I carry you up the steep stairs of the gang plank. And as you look around the little deck and inner lounge behind the pilot house, you light up. This boat is cool. You suddenly have a lot to say, and you want to explore and see all there is. We walk around the decks, climb the steep stairs, actually a ladder to the second deck, where there's another pilot's wheel and benches, enclosed in clear plastic walls. You're busy exploring every place you can get to.

We cruise out for four hours on the Bay. Your mother and I are uneasily wondering if four hours will be an eternity. The boat rolls like a slow elephant ride. But after a short while, all seems fine. We talk with friends, we eat hors d'oeuvres. You chow down on chicken brochettes. We go outside and see sea lions swimming beside us in the Bay. You're excited to see them.

We go outside the Gate, just underneath the great span of the Golden Gate Bridge. For a few moments the water is extremely choppy, and I'm thinking we're in for a bad ride now. But to my relief we return back under the bridge after only a few minutes. I'm pleased to see great freighters moving off into the twilight toward the Orient without us.

Darkness falls. The boat rolls. And then the sky explodes.

Fireworks are shooting off in brilliant colors all around us. Fireworks barges are emptying loads of gun powder and flying rockets into the air. You are in awe. Huge explosions are clapping around us. We smell sulphur and the air is misty with smoke.

You are pointing out skyrockets, mortars really, that are exploding in special designs, hearts, happy faces, circles with Saturn rings, even squares. You are in awe. This is so cool, you can hardly believe it. The fireworks show goes on and on, and you are pointing and shouting at the wonderful things you see.

Our little boat rolls, meanders, and cruises in the darkness. We aren't lost. We are in awe at an exploding sky. Wonder exists. You can feel it.

What Horses Eat

This morning you are dancing with Blackie, a large
stuffed horse with floppy legs, nearly as big as you are.
Yesterday, I did surgery on Blackie as I put 30 or so
stitches in his side to keep his internals internal. You
are waltzing Blackie as I come in the family room this
morning. You say cheerily, "Do you know what
Blackie had for breakfast?"

"What?" I ask.

You say, "Hay pie."

Wii Bowling

We're playing Wii Bowling, a computer game in which
you wave magic wands at the TV to make bowling
balls roll down the alley and knock down pins. It's
pretty realistic and fun, if you consider throwing a
heavy bowling ball by pointing a flashlight realistic.

You like it. When you approach your shot, you first
make a few aiming adjustments, pointing an orange
line down the lane at your intended pin victims. You
like to zoom in for a close-up view of the pins, just to

check where the ball is supposed to go. However, for all of us, when we throw, the ball most often takes an unusual curve at the last few seconds that whiffs past pins.

Once your throw is lined up, you swing the flashlight-remote control back, run, take a hippity hop, and swoosh your arm to the ceiling. The ball rolls calmly down the lane.

Strike!

Your mother and I eye each other amazed. You throw strike after strike as we struggle to get the evil spare splits. You throw two strikes in a row, then three; you learn the term "turkey" for making a three strike sequence. You're delighted to get a turkey.

Your mother and I realize we are way behind in the score. When the game ends, your score is 164, where your mom's is 132, and mine is 104.

I'm laughing each time you bowl, seeing your amazing success.

And I decide that I better bear down and practice. I need to get the Ryan technique down.

Your mother lines up her shot, runs, hippity hops, and strike!

I purse my lips and roll my eyes.

You're nearly a professional Wii bowler. I'm just a wobbly scarecrow to be laughed at. And you do.

Water Play at Gilroy Gardens

I realize that you like water. We go to an amusement park with rides, games, and gift shops. There are fountains, streams, and waterfalls everywhere. It's a garden amusement park, with families pushing strollers walking in shady avenues in hot hot weather. You are in your good flowery dress with sunglasses on. After riding a couple rides, we come to an area that is essentially walking behind a tumbling waterfall. It's drippy and wet. You jog under. You enjoy the sunny drizzle and dampening. We walk to another area for kids on hot days. It's a squirting menagerie where kids are walking around a playyard filled with flying water. Fountains suddenly squirt up from the ground like frightened clams. You quickly kick off your plastic Crocs and run into the crowd to explore the water works. Squirts erupt. Water drops on your head, fountains on your hunched back. You duck and stand, getting soaked. In two minutes, you are dripping like a pine tree in heavy rain, smiling and shrugging with the water. You're delighted. We go and eat lunch and you sit happily drenched like a wet mop. You eat your chicken tacos and in 15 minutes you're dry again. It's that hot. And we go walk under the waterfall again. Twice. You feel good in your skin. Especially with water all over it.

Boxing

We are boxing on the new Wii computer game. You hold a controller in each hand and start swinging. As your opponent, I do a few jabs and do a lot of ducking and weaving. You hit me and I say "Ouch!" You hit me a lot more times, and now I'm ouching like someone running barefoot across hot pavement. It makes you giggle to hear me. I start ouching like crazy until you're really laughing. Then you break into a tizzy of swings, laughing and punching your howling virtual dad. I get knocked out and lay down on the floor.

Laughing, you tell me you really love boxing. Your mother can hear the giggling from upstairs.

The Invention

You are beginning to live in your own world, filled with imagination. I look out this morning in the backyard and you are swinging high on the swing set by yourself. You are swinging in motion with yourself. You are in your own world.

A few weeks ago, you had me create a secret garden for you, under the olive tree in the front yard, hidden behind the thick agapanthus plants that make a green jungle wall. You planted carrots and various plants in your secret hideaway.

This morning you come to show me your new invention. I follow you to the dining room where a window overlooks your secret garden. The window is open slightly and a vacuum cleaner hose is reaching out the window down into the garden like a drooping boa. You have a flower watering can tied to the wall, and you put its spout into the hose, and water goes down to your secret garden and the thristy flowers. Your invention is a secret watering system that saves you time walking to the garden. You just pour water into the funneling hose. You enjoy filling a cup in the bathroom and walking several glasses of water over to your invention. It'll only take a million trips back and forth to get enough water out the window, and save all that time of walking one full watering can to the window and pouring it out.

Laziness, eagerness, and imagination are the flowers of invention. Whether it works or not.

If Ever

If ever I should leave you, and I will, someday, remember that life is about being you. The best and happiest you you can be. Don't think twice about going on and being you without me. Walk on. You can look back a bit, on some days, but don't linger, don't think your future is changed by any loss in your past. It's always there right in front of you. And it only depends on you. Which is a pretty marvelous thing. The person that I know you are. So go forward, do well, and that will be your gift to me, and to my ancestors who got me to you. Give the gift of the future to yourself. And it'll always be there for you, if ever you need it.

www.ingramcontent.com/pod-product-compliance
Lightning Source LLC
Chambersburg PA
CBHW052128090426
42741CB00009B/1994